Diva Dogs

A Style Guide to Living the
Fabulous Life

BY JO JO HARDER

Karla Austin, *Director of Operations & Product Development*
Nick Clemente, *Special Consultant*
Barbara Kimmel, *Editor in Chief*
Andrew DePrisco, *Developmental Editor*
Kerri Danskin, *Consulting Editor*
Kara Smith, *Production Supervisor*
Bill Jonas, *Designer*
Sheri Buhagiar, *Senior Graphic Artist*

Photographs courtesy of: cover, pp. 8, 17, 21, 23, 28, 33, 45, 52, 94, 115, 117, **David Pearlman, Absolute Image**; pp. 5, 6, 8, 10, 27, 30, 38, 41, 43, 47, 49, 51, 55, 59, 61, 62, 65, 67, 72, 73, 75–77, 79–81, 83, 85, 89, 91, 93, 97, 101, 102–104, 106, 108–111, 113, **Dean Payne, Picture This Productions**; pp. 9, 12 (top), 16, 18 (bottom), 24, 26, **A Pet's World**; p. 11 (left), 35 (bottom), 57, **Chien Coature**; pp. 11 (right), 92, **Gamboa Couture**; pp. 12 (bottom), 19, 22 (top and bottom), **Kaschi Duds**; pp. 13, 14 (top), 74, 100, **Monkey Daze**; pp. 14 (bottom), 15 (bottom), 18 (top), 31, 68, 95, **Dog Model/Corina Landa**; p. 15 (top), FouFou; p. 20 (top and bottom), **Manfred of Sweden/Björn Gärdsby**; p. 25, **Sckoon Organics**; p. 34, Christopher Appoldt; p. 35 (top), **Boutique of Paws**; pp. 36, 37, 98, **Total Diva Pets**; p. 105, **MODruff Sculpted Dogwear**

Location photographs courtesy of: Chateau Poochie ™, The Chesterfield Palm Beach, Jaguar Palm Beach, Marley's Palm Beach Collection, Sherry Frankel's Melangerie, Worth Avenue.

Library of Congress Cataloging-in-Publication Data

Harder, Jo Jo.
  Diva dogs : a style guide for living the fabulous life / by Jo Jo Harder.
    p. cm.
  ISBN-13: 978-1-933958-26-2
  ISBN-10: 1-933958-26-X
  1. Dogs—Pictorial works. 2. Dogs—Miscellanea. 3. Photography of dogs. I. Title.

  SF430.H37 2008
  636.7022'2—dc22
                          2008012670

BowTie Press®
A Division of BowTie, Inc.
23172 Plaza Pointe Dr., Ste. 230
Laguna Hills, California 92653

Printed and bound in China
13 12 11 10 09 08 1 2 3 4 5 6 7 8 9 10

Dedication

This book is lovingly dedicated to my son William Harder III and my friend Alma Hopkins, who relentlessly supported this book project from the start.

Thank you! Thank you! Thank you!

Acknowledgments

Sincere thanks to all of those at BowTie Press who share my vision and helped make this wonderful book possible.

Special thanks to my husband and son, William Harder II & III, my friend Alma Hopkins, Dean Payne, Carol Boker, Audra Barrett, Sherry Frankel, Amy and Molly Birkenes, Jean Landry, Todd Kozak, Lance Pain, Marley Herring, Arnelle Kendall, Amanda Garvey, and The Worth Avenue Association.

And to the dog models: Angel, Bullet, Daisy, Daphne Simone, Cole, Cookie, Fifey, Jaeger, Jersey, Jolly, Kody, Linda, Maya, Makaylah, Paige, Pumpkin, Riley, Romeo, Wiggles, and Wobbles.

—J.H.

The Publisher wishes to acknowledge the cooperation and courtesy of the following manufacturers for allowing us to include photographs of their fine pet products: A Pet's World, b.pet, Bellomania, Boutique of Paws, Chien Coature, Dog Model, FouFou Dog, K9Duds, Kaschi Duds, Lani—Dig Your Dog, Manfred of Sweden, Monkey Daze, Robbie Dawg, Sckoon Organics, Total Diva Pets, and Vince Gamboa.

—BowTie Press®

Contents

Introduction

We hear a lot about style these days, especially in my line of work as a fashion designer and stylist. Most people know what a fashion designer does, but not many are familiar with the work of a stylist. My definition of a stylist is "an expert with the Midas touch to make people, pets, objects, and events look fabulous." Our titles include hair stylist, make-up artist, celebrity stylist, window dresser, event planner, and fashion stylist. A stylist can work in various forums, from photo studios, film sets, and television stations to runways, designer studios, and fashion houses; from magazines, catalogs, and other print media to celebrities' homes, beauty salons, and day spas. And I thought I had done it all, until having a conversation with my friend Alma in Chicago. She informed me that dog parties are *hot* and suggested that I add them to my event styling list.

I grew up with dogs and have always been a huge dog fan. As I began to take notice of my surroundings here in Palm Beach County, I observed a dog grooming bus making its rounds in Boca Raton, an announcement for the Worth Avenue Pet Parade, and the first canine haute *parfum*, Oh My Dog! (from Belgium), at Saks Fifth Avenue in Palm Beach. My conclusion is that we really are living in dog daze!

Thus I wrote *Diva Dogs: A Style Guide to Living the Fabulous Life,* the ultimate style guide for those who wish to indulge their precious pooches. While developing this project, I had the pleasure of creating America's Top Dog Modeling Contest and my first doggy fashion photo shoot. The extraordinary doggy models from the photo shoot are featured throughout this book. One of the models is my own precious pooch Romeo, the handsome Italian Greyhound.

Diva Dogs not only showcases must-have fashions but also introduces the latest spa treatments and grooming aids, twenty-five rules of petiquette for various situations, and ideas for fifteen fabulous doggy parties that are certain to be the most sought-after invitations in town and country!

Enjoy

Chapter 1

Fashion Forward

W hen you're part of a high-class social circle, having the best wardrobe is an absolute necessity. What nonsense it is to think that all this time we've been asking our classy pooches to go naked! Fortunately, times are changing.

Right: In metallic formal wear, here's a Maltese who's used to setting trends.
Facing page: Looking like royalty is Linda, the first America's Top Dog Model winner.

Formal Wear

For a wedding or the Academy Awards, Fifi now has a choice between her crystal-encrusted coat and her lacy dress from the local boutique. And, of course, she's accessorizing without renting from Harry Winston's: a to-die-for pearl necklace, a traditional diamond, or a devastating rose-embellished collar? How is a girl to decide?

Manicured, bejeweled, and red-carpet ready.

Holiday Wear

Holiday fashion for pets has come a long way since the days when the most one could do was outfit a dog with reindeer antlers. Today's looks range from the classic human tradition of the Christmas sweater to faux fur to a sparkling blue coat for Hanukkah. Coordinating your dog's outfit with your own is easy with all of these options.

Happy Hanukkah from a stylin' Silky.

Keeping warm and jolly for Christmas in velvet and faux fur.

Rain Wear

Rain wear in the dog fashion world is coming down in buckets. It's all the rage with small and large dogs alike. From colorful parkas and rain bonnets to sleek yellow coats and matching booties and hats, a well-chosen ensemble can make the most of the dreariest days of the week. When fashion can serve multiple purposes—such as keeping a pooch dry and raising his owner's spirits at the same time—the designers are really fulfilling their mission. Not all dogs look dashing in goulashes, but some can pull them off (and not with their teeth!).

Camouflage rain wear keeps this attentive tot happy and dry.

Polka dots can make even rainy days seem bright.

Punk Wear

There are some dogs who have just never taken to ruffles, bows, and frills. For hardcore canine fashionistas, the punk look can be a great alternative. Studded collars, skull and crossbones T-shirts, and deconstructed styles for pets are catching on not only with tattoo artists and musicians but also with those who wouldn't dare to wear punk styles themselves but love to see them on their pets. Isn't it great to live out your fantasies through your Poodle?

Punkin' out in pink and denim.

 Casual Wear

There are a few key elements in a decent dog wardrobe. Just like humans, our furry friends need an ample supply of T-shirts, some in plain colors, and others with designs and slogans that express some personality.

If you're feeling lonely, a "My Mommy's Single" shirt on your dog, along with a walk in the park, may solve your problem. Feeling cranky? Throw the "I Bite" shirt on Buffy, and travel your neighborhood undisturbed. Variety is the key when you're putting this collection together. Doggy jeans come in handy, too, along with hoodies, sneakers, and sweaters.

A denim skirt and lots of l-o-v-e spells a casual fashion icon.

It's all about the fabrics and finishing touches.

Athletic Wear

While some dogs strut their stuff on the runway, earthier types prefer to show off by running full speed on the beach or joining their owners on challenging hikes. For the hardier types, more rugged gear is appropriate. Dogs' feet, however, are perfectly equipped for all kinds of athletic pursuits, so don't let them talk you into purchasing a pair of two-hundred-dollar running shoes or tennis sneakers! All-weather coats with reflective striping have been a standard for years for dogs who take nighttime walks, and these days they're a bit more stylish. These are also great for keeping your Lab warm after his swim in the ocean. If your athletic tendencies are more team-oriented, you'll find that your favorite sports team will almost certainly offer jerseys for dogs.

Ready for her morning jog, this Yorkie's ready to bust loose.

A sporty Chihuahua with strong ties to her Pittsburgh teams.

Beach Wear

Want to go to the beach with a friend who doesn't care if her derriere looks too accentuated in her new bikini? Bring your dog! These days there are countless bathing suit styles available for her, including stars and stripes for Independence Day, lovely lavender for a lazy June afternoon, and preppy polka dots for the pooch visiting Cape Cod. Fortunately, these bathing trunks aren't going to set you back as much as that Versace number you've been dieting for!

Don't forget the sunglasses and a terry cloth hoodie just in case that ocean breeze picks up. And ask your vet to recommend a good sunblock because your dog's skin is sensitive to the rays, too.

Left: "Take me any place with tropical weather and drinks!"
Facing page: Daisy, sunning herself in Boca Raton.

Protective Outerwear

Protection from the cold is important for dogs, especially single-coated ones. Fortunately, the style options in this category are boundless. You can't beat a faux-fur-lined parka for warmth and protection from damp weather, but for chilly fall days, your best bet is a thick cable-knit sweater. Where there is snow, especially in the cities, there is bound to be salt, which can cause cracked paw pads, so make sure you protect your dog's feet with a pair of booties or sneakers.

In stormy weather, a hood can be a dog-send.

For summer days at the shore, a sweater's ideal for those afternoon ocean breezes.

A nylon parka with good insulation keeps the cold and drafts out.

Ready for the Oscars and the red carpet commentators.

A civilized afternoon for a sail.

Greyhound is the way to go!

 Sleep Wear

If you spent about half your life sleeping, as your dog does, don't you think you might want some stylish jammies? Especially considering the fact that the floor of a house is typically several degrees cooler than the temperature that the humans are enjoying higher up, your dog will certainly welcome a nice set of flannel pajamas. Why not coordinate your dog's look with a matching set for yourself?

A sassy Chihuahua, pretty in pink and ready for bed.

A terry bathrobe for a smooth Teckel.

Costume **Wear**

For all those grown-ups who feel silly dressing up for Halloween but secretly miss all the fun, dressing up a dog is a great alternative. Keep sizing very firmly in mind as you choose because costumes tend to be a little more complex than regular dog clothing. But have a ball dressing up your Chihuahua as a crocodile or your Pug as a prisoner.

Jaeger hopes none of his Pug pals recognizes him at the party.

 Winter Wear

It's always so tough to look stylish in the winter when you have to wear such a heavy coat all the time, isn't it? Once again, your dog comes to the rescue by trotting at your side in a coordinated sweater and scarf set or a fabulous leather coat. While you're trying to figure out how to manage your coat and your wine at that winter cocktail party, your dog is a sitting sophisticate in her pink faux-fur stole.

A wintry ensemble to turn heads.

Green

An increased focus on environmental responsibility has encouraged many pet fashion companies to make garments and accessories with organic materials. Dressing your dog in "green" gives you a lighthearted way to bring up the topic of preservation, and you'll notice that your little activist looks great, too!

No matter what color you're wearing, think green!

The Accessories

Everyone knows that what separates human from beast is human's ability to accessorize! Thus, we humans must present our canine charges with the very best in accessories. Dog owners have never had as many fabulous options as they do today—from rhinestone-studded collars and purple leather leashes to tiaras, earrings, and faux-fur wraps, not to mention any of the truly frivolous fashion accessories!

Collars and Leashes

Solid-color nylon is *so* last century. These days, you can coordinate your dog's leash and collar with your shoes and purse so you'll both look fabulous. For spunky dogs that won't put up with clothes or shoes, a collar can be a great way to give them some style.

A matching harness and leash can give a dog panache and confidence on the runway or Main Street.

Bows and Headgear

We all love Lola's wild Yorkie hairdo, but sometimes it just needs to be a little bit more under control. A sparkly pink bow gets her ready for any party, and it couldn't be easier to use. Doggy boutiques offer a variety of great bows, barrettes, and other stylish clip-ons to spice up a pooch who's having a mediocre hair day. For true diva dog occasions, a tiara raises the spirits of your royal charge and all her adoring subjects.

A stylish visor blocks the sun and complements perky ears.

Protective Eyewear

Protection from the sun's rays is important, but there's no denying that the main reason to wear sunglasses is that they look cool. The same holds true when the sunglasses are on a dog. Unlike years ago, when people tried balancing human shades on their furry friends, today's canine sunglasses have straps in all the right places to keep them in place.

Kody says, "Come chill with one cool dog down in Margaritaville."

Head Wear

If your dog won't wear sunglasses, a hat can be a great option for keeping the sun out of his eyes during that walk on the beach. Today's caps for dogs have visors and ear holes that keep them on your dog's head.

Straw coordinates, as modeled by Riley, never lose their appeal.

Pink herringbone is all the rage in Paris this spring!

Scarves and Bandannas

With a snap or other type of fastening for safety, a scarf or bandanna can be a fabulous accessory for a dog and a great way to fight a chill. Scarves can be stylish in any season, and bandannas can add a touch of color to any ensemble.

This young lady is ready to plunder and pillage many hearts.

Jewelry and Charms

Although probably not a good risk to take on a large dog, jewelry can be adorable on a toy breed. A delicate necklace gives her the sophisticated look she needs to accompany you to the most formal occasion. Larger dogs can enjoy the trend with jeweled charms, which can be attached to their collars.

A diva most days, Fifey is a princess on weekends only.

Dog Carriers

Now designed with style and stealth in mind, today's carriers look more like designer handbags than animal transportation devices. Metallic ones are particularly versatile, as silver and gold can coordinate with any look. Be careful to consider your pooch's comfort first, though! It's great to be able to sneak your dog into the movie theater with you, but ample space and air are imperative.

A great way to tour Fifth Avenue.

Party

Without a doubt the most popular canine accessory, the party collar gives a dog instant style. These collars are affordable and come in styles ranging from punk to formal to simply hilarious, and they're easily tolerated by dogs who are accustomed to wearing collars.

A bold fashion statement will be the talk of the doggy party.

Decked out for the birthday-party circuit.

Dog Wigs

Is it possible for an owner to go too far before her friends accuse her of wigging out? Never! Owners can live out some of their own fantasies through their willing diva dogs. If you've always wanted to spend an evening in Donna Summer's shoes or to find out if platinum blondes really feel dumber, you can live that moment vicariously through your pooch. Dog wigs can make an ordinary owner's big-hair dreams come true!

A natural strawberry blonde, no doubt.

"Last chance for love!"

Blondes have more fun, a lot more!

Chapter 2

Entertaining Canine Style

Dogs are party animals! They have a sociable nature just as people do. Doggy parties provide an opportunity for canine friends to share yappy occasions and to celebrate milestones.

You do not need a grand doghouse to entertain. You are not even required to be a great cook, thanks to the many wonderful doggy delis and bakeries around the country today. The key ingredients are organization, imagination, and presentation!

First, to get organized, make a list of the key essentials to any fabulous gathering: type of party, date, time, location, number of guests, decorations, music, activity, and menu. Next, imagine the type of setting you would like to portray and create a theme. Keep the three Bs in mind: Be creative. Be silly. Be extravagant. Finally, develop the theme with special elements, such as themed invitations, paw-shaped cuisine, and doggy bags filled with canine treats and toys.

The success of a doggy party is in the details. Here I share my insight and guidance for hosting fifteen fabulous doggy parties. The tail-wagging celebrations discussed on the following pages are easy to create and will bring out the party animal in any pooch and his owner.

Facing page: Tea for four!

Birthday Party

Make your doggy's wish come true by creating a fairy-tale birthday party! The first thing for a good party host to do is to decide on a theme. If you're stumped for ideas, have a chat with the owner of your favorite pet-related business. Chances are, she's heard it all and can give you some great material to choose from. The theme selected for our sample canine-style party is Camp Snoopy.

The Setting

Here's how to create a Camp Snoopy birthday party in your backyard. (This is an outdoor party idea. For cool weather, you may have to rent indoor space.)

Since this is a birthday party, you may choose either your pooch's actual birth date or the date that he became a part of your family (the adoption date).

A good time frame for this party is noon to three o'clock, which allows sufficient time for eating, socializing, and activities. In the warmer months you may want to start later in the afternoon, when it's cooler, to avoid unnecessary panting.

The setting for Camp Snoopy consists of a white tent set up in the backyard, in a rented space, or on a covered patio. Festoon the entrance to your home and the patio area and party tent with red, black, and white (Snoopy colors) balloons, for dramatic contrast.

Canine guests can include friends in the neighborhood, your favorite doggy spa pals, or regular play-mates. Make certain that all the canine guests you invite get along with people and other dogs. You may have to screen the dogs to make sure that their temperaments are party ready. Avoid dogs that are overly spoiled, greedy, or pushy. Sloppy eaters can also cast a pall over an otherwise tasteful canine gathering.

Remember to invite the owners along with their dogs, and include them in your guest count. It's unavoidable. If you select your doggy invitees with care, however, you needn't worry about the owners' party-ready temperaments.

Facing page: Charming Poodles Paige and Jersey guard the loot.

It's rare to find a well-behaved dog who's owned by an overbearing know-it-all. Nice dogs are usually owned by nice people, and obnoxious, unruly dogs owned by people who would never make Mrs. Astor's Four Hundred. Human guests can also include family members and friends who are known to be both dog lovers and well trained.

The Menu and Activities

Now for the menu! Coordinate the menu with the theme of your doggy party. Remember when planning the menu that like people, some dogs have food allergies. Be sure to check with your guests to find out if any of their canine escorts have special dietary concerns.

It wouldn't be a Snoopy party without a Snoopy doghouse cake! If you're a little Martha Stewart (or have a friend who is), you can bake this yourself; otherwise, you might as well spend a fortune at the local bakery. If you're not whipping up a fabulous canine confection at home, place your order at a doggy bakery for your Snoopy doghouse cake and any snacks, such as cheese treats, you'd like to serve your four-legged guests. At your local people bakery,

Snoopy's always the life of the party!

or perhaps the supermarket, place an order for a Snoopy-themed cake for your human guests. Fancy finger sandwiches (small enough to pass to the canine companions) and a fruit platter (no grapes!) can be ordered from a caterer or a supermarket. For a true festive occasion for the dogs, you'll need to include champagne (that's what dogs imagine bottled water to be; Evian without the fizz is the best). Watch tails wag when the guests see this spread!

Since Snoopy is into bones, as are most self-respecting dogs, plan activities such as fetch and race for the bone.

Countdown

Four to six weeks before the party—there's nothing spontaneous about this event, as good parties take lots of time to plan—design the invitation and send it to the printer. If you're handy with your computer, you can print the invitations yourself.

Three weeks before the party, send out invitations. Tie a Snoopy invitation to a doggy bone and send special delivery.

Two weeks before the party, purchase balloons and make or purchase miniature white bone-shaped confetti. For your place settings, buy red personalized doggy bowls for each canine guest and black place mats to set the bowls on. Get white gift bags and stuff them with red, black, and white paw print tissue paper, a doggy toy, and a treat for each canine guest. Make sure the bags are big enough to hold the personalized bowls, which you'll also send home with the guests. Don't forget party favors for your human guests. A pet-themed photo frame for displaying their favorite party photo can be a great idea. You should also buy doggy bones for the games.

One week before the party, confirm RSVPs and place your orders for food and desserts.

On the morning of the party, pitch the party tent. Pick up the cake and snacks at the doggy bakery, then pick up the people cake, sandwiches, and fruit platter.

Once you're home, prepare the tent. Inside the tent, set black place mats in a circle, one for each canine guest. On each mat, set a red doggy bowl. On a round table in the middle of the circle, place the doggy bags and Snoopy doghouse cake. Be sure to have cleanup materials such as paper towels, wipes, and baggies readily available.

For the human guests, set a table, buffet style, on the patio. Cover the table with a black tablecloth and sprinkle with bone-shaped confetti. Arrange red paper plates, cutlery, and napkins. Put out the cake, sandwiches, fruit, and sparkling flavored water after guests arrive.

Entertaining Canine Style

Party Time!

The birthday pooch should be at your side to greet guests as they arrive.

Serve lunch after all guests have arrived. Position each canine guest at a designated place mat and serve the cheese treats. Once the bowls are empty, fill them up with doggy champagne.

Direct human guests to help themselves to the buffet, which should be set out while doggies are lapping up their libations.

Now on to the activities! Adults can get involved in doggy activities or, if of a more sedentary disposition, relax and chat while their companions chase around. If there are children, they may enjoy participating in doggy activities.

Provide a bone for each doggy, and play free-for-all fetch. For the dog races, rent a tunnel for dogs to race through. Have lots of bone treats to offer the winners.

As each guest departs, hand out the white doggy bags containing the red personalized doggy bowl, the doggy toy and treat, and the party favor for your human friends. Doggies will pant for the contents and have fond memories for many dog days to come!

Party Themes

- Blue's Clue
- Clifford the Big Red Dog
- 101 Dalmatians
- Wishbone

Facing page: Kody's announcing that it's party time.

Doggy Valentine's Tea

What better way to express puppy love on Valentine's Day than by having a romantic afternoon tea?

The Setting

Prepare the tea party in a garden or create an intimate setting at a doggy dig, such as a pet resort, doggy day care, or dog bakery. Tea at a doggy dig would be most convenient since the catering is on-site. This will allow you to relax and enjoy quality time with friends. Do, however, get involved in initial preparations to ensure that all will be perfect, dahling!

Decorate using a pink and white color scheme. White linen tablecloths centered by pink roses would be positively romantic. A spring garden makes a lovely setting for a tea as well. The flowers in full bloom provide impeccable decoration. A colorful blanket serves as a comfortable table setting for canine guests. People guests can enjoy their tea at a table set traditionally, with fine linen, china, crystal, and silver. Select appropriate music for the party: light British pop or classical music would be a nice touch.

Keep the guest list at an intimate total of twelve—that's six dogs with six people. If you have a friend who has two mannerly dogs, you can gain some floor space by including the trio (and one fewer human to feed!). Schedule the event at four o'clock, and request that all guests come dressed for tea. Four weeks before the tea, send out your homemade heart-shaped invitations.

The Menu and Activities

Serve a variety of canapés, petits fours, champagne, and tea for the human guests. Here's a doggy menu that embraces romance: lady paws, carob doggy kisses, heart-shaped peanut butter cookies, and liverwurst canapés. Check out any special treats the dog bakery has for the holiday, too. For beverages, how about a varietal from Bark Vineyards? Real gourmet doggy wines, such as Barkundy, Sauvignon Bark, or Pinot Leasheo, will add panache to a Valentine's get-together. Have plenty of heart-shaped treats available for the activities, including contests for best behavior—best sit, stay, and paw shake!

Facing page: "Don't drool on the doily, darling."

Tea Party Advice

- Dogs may enjoy drinking tea. It's no worse for their teeth than it is for yours.

- Inviting dogs of British descent makes infinitely more sense than inviting canines of American or German lineage. The Britons, after all, invented afternoon teas—as well as most of the good dog breeds. Think Cavalier King Charles Spaniels, Bulldogs, and any toy terrier. You're always safe inviting Pugs and French Bulldogs, although both can become flatulent if they overeat.

- Proper decorum, attire, and etiquette are critical to a formal afternoon tea. Don't compromise simply because you're inviting dogs. Some dogs can be insulted by an invitation to an informal tea party. Remember what happened in Boston.

Facing page: Daisy takes no prisoners.

Doggy Spa Party

Invite your best canine friends for a day of pampering at your favorite doggy spa or grooming salon. Work with the aestheticians on preparations for your spa party. Make guests feel welcome by creating a total experience. Consider sights, smells, and other sensations. Make certain that each station is set up with spa treatments that you have ordered. Provide a group of comfortable cushions where everyone can relax. See that fragrant candles (inaccessible to any canine guests) are placed throughout the spa and that lighting is adjusted for relaxation. Provide terry cloth robes for guests, and order a healthy lunch for all.

Remember, it's the details that make all the difference!

Plan your spa party from 11 a.m. to 3 p.m.

Here is a sample itinerary:

11:00–11:15	Guests arrive
11:15–11:45	Doga (yoga for dogs)
11:45–12:30	Special treatment bath
12:30–1:15	Spa lunch
1:15–1:45	Styling and ribbons
1:45–2:15	Pedicure for pets
2:15–2:45	Massage
2:45–3:00	Refreshments

Facing page: A "spa-tacular" outing is underway.

Cocktail Party

Cocktail parties are great for entertaining canine style, as they are fun and simple to plan. The joy of cocktail parties is that they can be put together at a moment's notice. You also can entertain small or large groups of guests.

The Setting

The right mix of doggy guests, tasty appetizers, glowing candles, and jazzy sounds is essential for scoring a successful cocktail party. You can purchase invitations or, if you're the artsy type, make your own. If you are too busy to send invitations by mail, a telephone call would be fine.

Cole and Cookie, sharing some bubbly and good chatter.

Safety Tips

- Do not serve dogs chocolate, Belgian or otherwise. It's hazardous to their health and expensive, too!
- Place lighted candles in secure areas inaccessible to pets and small children.

If you are fortunate to have appropriate indoor space for entertaining canine and human guests, then you can confidently plan parties inside year-round. Otherwise, plan the cocktail party outdoors, where doggy friends can mingle and romp freely.

If you want your party to benefit a local shelter or another animal organization, it's a great idea to ask your local doggy bakery or boutique to partner with you in the effort for your paying guests. These businesses often host "yappy hours." The partnership will allow you to take advantage of the shop's great location, and the business owner would likely be willing to piggyback the event into the advertising she's already planning.

The Menu and Activities

Buffet and bite-size food work best at cocktail parties, and champagne is always in style. Provide separate drink bowls for each canine guest. Serve doggy champagne (bottled water) to your canine partiers and the real "bubbly" or favorite beverage to their people. Have a full bar set up where people can help themselves, or hire a bartender. This cocktail party menu is suitable for all guests and delicious!

- Pigs-in-a-blanket
  (these are really little dogs!)
- Turkey meatballs
- Stuffed zucchini
- Steamed carrot nibbles
- Cheese tray with multigrain biscuits
- Peanut butter paws
- Carob truffles

Doggies will want to romp and roll, so select upbeat pet sounds to keep the party lively! Set a buffet table with desserts when the party starts to wind down. It's a polite way of letting guests know the cocktail party is coming to an "end!"

Dog Party Music

Dog-themed parties can be given a leg up by fun albums and songs that reference our canine friends. Likewise there are a number of music companies now producing discs designed with dogs' aural taste in mind. Many are enjoyable for humans, too, and you might find a good one at your favorite pet boutique. Here are some of the author's fave human tunes for dog parties:

"Blame It on the Dog"	Thompson Brothers Band
"Blue's Clues Theme Song"	
"Gonna Buy Me a Dog"	The Monkees
"Hound Dog"	Elvis Presley
"How Much Is That Doggy in the Window?"	Patti Page
"Me and You and a Dog Name Boo"	Lobo
"My Dog's Bigger Than Your Dog"	Tom Paxton
"Pet Sounds"	The Beach Boys
"Puppy Love"	Paul Anka
Songs to Make Dogs Happy	Kim Ogden
Tails of the City	Murray Weinstock
Three Dog Night: Complete Hit Singles	Three Dog Night
"Walking the Dog"	Rufus Thomas
"Who Let the Dogs Out"	Baha Men
"Wishbone Theme Song"	

Facing page: Maya admits, "Disco is my middle name."

Doggy Debutante Ball

A doggy debutante ball, or a canine cotillion, is a means of presenting a young lady (in this case, a bitch in training) to society.

The Setting

To step into a society as a debutante is an honor seeped in tradition; therefore, you may want to form a committee to help host this event. Long before this special evening draws near, consider your doggy's escort, grooming details, and formal wear.

Diva dog dresses do not have to be white, but do choose cuts that will complement your young dog's developing figure. Add a tiara and some sensible evening jewelry for a regal touch! Tuxedos are the expected attire for all male dog escorts. Luckily, most dog boutiques offer a wide range of stylish formal wear.

The Menu and Activities

This should be a catered event, with separate dining areas set up for canines and their people. Select a doggy location that caters to both humans and canines.

The following menu can be adapted for all attendees, two- and four-footed.

- Choice of roast prime sirloin of beef or boneless turkey breast
- Oven-roasted potatoes
- Grilled vegetables
- Carrot cake

The ball begins with the formality of each young lady and her partner being presented to the guests. Usually, as each couple walks the length of the ballroom's red carpet, an emcee comments about the lady's dress, her hobbies, and perhaps her favorite kibble.

Once all the young ladies have been presented, the group moves in a formation and performs two or three formal dances. At a doggy ball, the diva in the making would have to dance with her owner, since canine escorts rarely are light on their toes. The presentation and the dance are the official part of the proceeding. The dances are followed by a sit-down meal and more freestyle dancing for everyone.

Facing page: For this dapper escort, the more spangles, the better.

Graduation Open House

Graduating from obedience school is an important milestone in any doggy's life. Your precious darling is now a "well-heeled" grad and should be treated as such.

The Setting

A graduation party is an opportunity to celebrate a job well done and toast a positively bright future. The graduate is one of a kind, so plan this special day with personalized creations. Make a guest list including the family, friends, and classmates. Mail invitations with your doggy's graduation photo and paw print.

This should be an outdoor event. (You know how rowdy recent graduates can be!) If you do not have a covered patio, then rent a big tent.

Set up a table displaying the life of your dog from puppy stage to present. Use photos, videos, keepsake items, graduation cap, and diploma. Display a cardboard cutout dog, so guests can sign it and leave congratulatory notes for the graduate.

Decorate with balloons representing your doggy's school colors. Stamp balloons with paw prints.

Stamp or purchase brown doggy bags with paw prints, fill them with doggy treats, and offer them as party favors. Activities are really not necessary at a graduation open doghouse.

The Menu and Activities

Plan a stress-free buffet menu by ordering party trays from your local supermarket. Doggies and people both will enjoy cheeses and biscuits, deviled eggs, meatballs, assorted cold cuts, and seedless watermelon slices without the rinds. At your local dog bakery, order a personalized sheet cake with a photo of your dog wearing a graduation cap. Order peanut butter paw cookies or some other delish invention as well. For the doggies, serve water; for everyone else, serve lemonade, iced tea, and soda. Select paper goods and decorations with a paw print theme.

This is a time to relax, enjoy good food and company, and look to the future. Take lots of photos of this very special day! Better yet, hire a local pet photographer to capture each grad in cap and gown.

Facing page: The happy grad, Romeo's got brains and the paperwork to prove it.

Unleashed Park Picnic

A picnic is a fun way to enjoy an unfettered romp in the park with three to five close canine friends. In recent years, there has been a rise in the number of dog parks. This is good news for doggies, as what fun is a picnic if you are confined to a leash?

The Setting

Whether the picnic is as simple as a few biscuits in a doggy bag or a sumptuous spread, there is always something special about eating in the open air. The picnic setting should be bright and multihued to complement nature. Bring colorful blankets for doggies and their people. What's important is that all guests relax and enjoy delicious fare prior to the unleashing.

Items to pack for your picnic:
- Doggy bowls
- Paper plates
- Plastic glasses
- Serving utensils
- Napkins
- Paper towels
- Insect repellent
- Sunblock
- Trash bags

The Menu

Like kids, doggies will delight in simple basic fare such as peanut butter or egg salad sandwiches. The smell of mashed peanuts or eggs guarantees tails wagging! For human picnickers, a more sophisticated option is country style pâté, which your guests can eat on crispy water crackers. (Let's not share the pâté with the pooches, as it's rich and fatty—too good to waste even on a diva dog.) Be sure to keep any perishable foods chilled while outdoors. Carob cookies are a perfect doggy picnic dessert. In the summertime, nothing beats watermelon as a refreshing finale—serve it seedless and without the rind. (Be aware that some fruits such as grapes and raisins are toxic to dogs, and double-check before making a selection.) Guests will be thirsty, so bring limeade for people and plenty of water for doggies. And although laws may prohibit humans from consuming certain party beverages in public places, these laws don't apply to dogs! Look into Bowser Beer for doggy beer and Bark Vineyards for doggy wines.

So that you're not too stressed on picnic day, do your prep work the

Wobbles and Wiggles, enjoying a sunny picnic outing.

day before. For example, the egg salad and limeade can be made a day in advance. Slice up the watermelon the night before, carefully removing the seeds and the rind. Assemble the sandwiches the morning of the picnic—not even dogs like soggy bread. The rest of the preparation involves packing items to travel. Wrap sandwiches in plastic wrap. Pack watermelon slices and cookies in airtight containers. Load all food into a cooler. Transport limeade in an insulated thermos. Pack the nonperishable items in a large wicker basket, which you can decorate to add to the festive tone of the proceedings.

Doggies' Night Out

If your pooch loves to play, an unleashed picnic in the park with lots of frolic, Frisbee, and fetch can be a fun way to spend the afternoon! Invite a friend or two, or three, for "doggies' night out." Girls and dogs, who wanna have fun, will always enjoy a "night out." This is an opportunity to get together with girlfriends and their pooches with little fuss and lots of fizz.

This spontaneous gathering requires a free night and a few phone calls to your BFFs who own diva pooches. Be sure you have a nice bottle of white wine or prosecco on ice, or some sparkling water or cider, plus some bottled water for the pooches. If you're really feeling decadent, how about inventing your own martini—the cosmopawlitan, the yappletini, or the dirty dogtini?

If you're lucky enough to live in a community where dogs are welcome at an outdoor café or restaurant, make that a destination for "doggies' night out." In most cities, you can take your pooch shopping with you, especially if he's small enough to tuck in your Coach bag. Look for pet-oriented events that might make for a fun outing. Have a definite plan so that the evening flows as effortlessly as the bubbly and gin. A word to the sober: don't get too tipsy while out on the town with Tipper and your friends. Keep safety and the road in front of you in focus.

Jolly shops at Marley's Palm Beach Collection.

Popular

- Walk your doggies along a popular avenue, and grab a bite to eat at an outdoor café.
- Get takeout and enjoy it on a dog-friendly beach while watching the sunset.
- Visit an outdoor shopping center—stroll, window shop, and dog watch, then have a light dinner at a dog-friendly restaurant.
- Pack a picnic dinner and venture over to a pooch-welcoming park that offers live entertainment—spread out a blanket, relax, and enjoy!
- Visit the local pet boutique's "yappy hour," where you're bound to run into some single dawgs and their dogs. The best thing about these events is that the cute guys you meet are all dog lovers (and, one hopes, unleashed).

Puppy Shower

Your friend is having a puppy! This is a good cause for a celebration! And you are the dear friend who has decided to host the shower. Here's some helpful guidance to pull off a flawless party, one that will create a memorable impression for your friend and guests.

The Setting

Make certain to select a date that the new mom has free. A weekend afternoon is the most appropriate time for a shower, which typically lasts three hours. Ask her for a guest list of people she would like to invite.

Set a date to escort the new puppy owner to her favorite pet boutique, where she can select her registry items. These can range from essentials (such as collars and leashes) to luxuries such as spa products, fancy beds, and cutting-edge doggy fashions.

Send invitations to the puppy shower a month in advance. The theme of the shower, perhaps inspired by the new puppy's breed, can be incorporated into the invitation. For example, if your friend is adopting an Asian breed, such as a Shih Tzu, a Lhasa Apso, or a Pug, you can introduce Chinese characters to the design. Create your own invitation using a doggy illustration or actual photo of the new puppy. Invitations with a puppy theme can also be purchased at an upscale stationer or a fun online store. The invitation should include the following information:

- Name(s) of puppy and parent(s) being honored
- Date, time, and location of the shower
- Name of the person giving the shower
- Whom guests can bring—kids, dogs, spouses, or partners
- How to RSVP
- Deadline to RSVP
- Name of local boutique where the guest of honor is registered

The location of the shower depends on the guest list. If only people will be attending, the shower can easily be held in your home. If

Facing page. Wobbles, in her spring ensemble, is the toast of the puppy shower.

pets are invited, it may be more convenient to select a doggy dig and have the event catered.

To decorate a room following a puppy theme, here are a few guidelines. Place a diaper and bib on a big stuffed dog. Tie a bunch of colorful balloons around it, and set it in a chair. Place an autograph doggy in the center of the gift table, so guests can sign it and the new pup can have it as a keepsake. On the central food table, place a toy doggy holding a bouquet of flowers. Position a pastel-colored umbrella above the new mom's chair, so she can be "showered in style."

The Menu and Activities

The shower's puppy theme can be further developed through the decorations, the activities, and the menu. Naturally, for the arrival of the aforementioned Shih Tzu, a fancy Chinese buffet would be lovely. If the puppy is a good all-American mutt, then casual fun fare; red, white, and blue decorations; and naturally blonde waiters would be perfect.

Keep the menu simple. The type of food to serve will depend on the time of day. Midday or early evening should include a meal, whereas a shower after 6 o'clock could be dessert only. Select food that is easy to eat, and serve it buffet style. Here is a menu suggestion: miniature quiche, fresh fruit kabobs, assorted canapés, sandwiches, animal crackers, ice cream, cake, and punch. Use a metal doggy-shaped cookie cutter to cut canapés. Make or purchase a doggy-shaped cake at your local bakery.

Select games with a puppy theme for activities. For instance, when guests arrive, provide each one with a clothespin to clip to her collar or lapel. If a guest hears someone saying the word *puppy* at any time during the course of the shower, the hearer can take the offender's clothespin and clip it on her own collar. The guest with the most clothespins at the end of the shower wins a door prize.

Another great game to play is puppy shower bingo. To play this spin on a traditional bridal shower game, you will need to print out blank bingo cards. Place a bingo card and a pen or pencil at each

Facing page: Like everyone else, Romeo wonders, "Who let the dogs out?"

A toasty pair of pajamas to guarantee sweet puppy dreams.

Gift

Puppy bowl with a fashionable design
Puppy collar and leash
Decorative photo frame
Rubber rattle (chew toy)
Stuffed dog toy
PetsCELL (a waterproof cell phone optimized for dogs)
Raincoat and boots
Cashmere sweater
Pup tent
Doggy dream house
Grooming sprays
Gourmet treats
Training manual or a breed book

guest's seat. You'll instruct the guests to fill in the blank squares by writing the names of items that they think the new mom and her four-legged little one will receive as shower gifts (such as a collar, dog bed, sweater, vacation in the Bahamas). As the gifts are opened, the guests will mark an X through any square that contains the name of a gift. The first person to get an entire vertical, horizontal, or diagonal line will, of course, exclaim "Bingo!" and receive a fabulous door prize. Continue playing until the next person gets bingo, and so on. Have five door prizes on hand for the first five people who win.

For another prize-giving opportunity (and there can never be too many of those), place a puppy sticker under one of the guests' plates before people arrive. After everyone has finished eating, tell the guests to check the bottom of their plates. The guest with the puppy sticker wins the door prize. It's always fun for people to win prizes, and they do not have to be extravagant ones. Purchase useful items for prizes, such as doggy treats, a rubber bone, a doggy brush, and wag bags.

Serve the desserts after all the gifts have been opened or after the meal has been eaten, indicating that the shower has come to an end.

Backyard Bark-B-Q

A backyard Bark-B-Q is the perfect casual gathering for doggies, neighbors, family, and friends. It is also the perfect space for organizing doggy races and other canine activities. And, there is nothing more inviting than the aroma of food cooking on a grill.

The Setting

It's always fun to have a theme for your Bark-B-Q. For instance, if you are planning to celebrate a holiday such as Independence Day, Memorial Day, or Labor Day, you can develop a patriotic setting using a red, white, and blue color scheme for table settings, flowers, invitations, and menu. Create an archway over the entrance to your home or backyard, using red, white, and blue balloons tied together with lots of ribbons. Ask guests to wear red, white, and blue attire to complete the picture. Have a red, white, and blue bandanna ready for each invited pooch.

Another fun idea is to create a Hollywood hoedown. Invite guests to wear western attire embellished with sequins or rhinestones. Include accessories such as a ten-gallon hat, boots or high top sneakers, and kerchiefs. Dress the doggies western style, too!

Details matter even for outdoor entertaining. Set the table using a red and white checked tablecloth and napkins. Fill a wheelbarrow with ice for chilled beverages and watering cans with wild flowers. If possible, use bales of hay for seating.

Safety Tips

- Keep small children and doggies away from lit grills.
- Have a fire extinguisher or a large box of baking soda on hand in case of a grill flare-up.
- Meats should be cooked to destroy parasites. Let the meat cool down to room temperature before serving to dogs.
- Never give your dog chicken or turkey bones. They contain splinters that can cause serious side effects. Cooked bones are more likely to splinter than uncooked ones are.

The Menu and Activities

Whatever the occasion, remember to keep it simple and casual. A backyard Bark-B-Q is the ultimate relaxed get-together and an uncomplicated menu will set the tone for a dog day filled with good times!

The grilled foods are always the centerpiece for a backyard Bark-B-Q. Canine tails will wag for hot dogs, hamburgers, and steak, especially if you dress them up with a gourmet gravy made for dogs. Doggies will also get a nose and earful when corn on the cob is sizzling on the grill. The most popular side dishes at a Bark-B-Q are potato salad, coleslaw, and baked beans. Have plenty of water on hand for doggies and raspberry lemonade and sangria for their people. Serve good old-fashioned desserts such as apple pie or peach cobbler and vanilla ice cream for your human guests. For canine guests, consider gourmet doggy ice cream or ice pudding, available from local or online pet boutiques. For the most part, this menu is for eating off paper plates, which make outdoor entertaining easier. So grab a cold drink, put on the music, and fire up the grill!

Left: Romeo patiently awaits his well-done cheeseburger.
Facing page: It's every Poodle for himself at this Bark-B-Q! Jersey helps himself to the first 'dog off the grill.

Dog Days Pool Party

When we hear the phrase "dog days of summer," August and September usually come to mind. We envision sweltering hot afternoons, with horses sweating, men perspiring, women glowing—and dogs panting. Feeling the heat? Invite friends and their pooches for a doggone cool afternoon in the pool!

The Setting

Doggies will love to bark, wiggle, and splash with their people in the pool! If you don't have a pool, befriend a dog lover who does and convince him or her that a doggy pool party is a very cool thing. (Alternatively, you can just turn the page to the next party.)

Send an invitation with an illustration of you and your pooch wearing matching T-shirts and sunglasses, standing under a blazing sun. Since it's a pool party, you could create a swell invitation using watercolor. Be sure to mail invitations in colorful envelopes. Include the date, time, and place; remind everyone that it's BYOB (bring your own bones).

Make a welcome sign for guests that says "It's a Dog Days of Summer Pool Party—Come Cool Your Paws!"

Left: Arrive to the pool party with summer flair—
a gingham sundress never goes out of style.
Facing page: Margaritas poolside make for the perfect dog-day social.

The Menu and Activities

Keep it cool and simple. Use paper goods with a fun dog theme. Set up a buffet with three types of salad, such as chicken Caesar, pasta, and fruit. Sandwiches can be fun and elegant, especially if you have a large paw- or bone-shaped cutter to customize the sandwiches. Use fresh ingredients in the sandwiches, such as avocado, bean sprouts, and heirloom tomatoes. Remove veggies from the sandwiches before sharing them with any four-pawed beggars. Don't forget the doggies' bone-shaped cheese snacks and beef jerky treats.

For dessert, all guests will enjoy apple-cinnamon cake. Blueberry pie with cinnamon ice cream is another no-fail dessert for your human guests.

What to pour? Champagne (bottled water) for doggies and strawberry margaritas for their people.

The activities? Swimming and lounging by the pool!

Left: A touch of elegance is always appreciated.
Facing page: Wiggles enjoys the Palm Beach.

"Tail" Gate Party

Spring and summer aren't the only seasons to entertain outdoors, as this autumnal party scores high marks in the end zone. Doggies will enjoy the crisp autumn air and colorful leaves of the countryside. Everything smells great in the fall, and there are always unexpected joys when rolling in a pile of fallen leaves.

The Setting

You do not necessarily have to attend a football game to tailgate, but if you choose to do so, get there early to find a good spot. Part of the fun is having an area where doggies can play the field, so park next to a grassy area or at the end of a parking row. This will allow more room for serious "tail" gating!

Dress yourself and your doggy in team colors if you plan to tailgate at a football game. To help your guests find you, fly a flag in your team's colors from a high pole. If you decide to bypass the football game and take in the countryside, as many owners of diva dogs might opt to do, be sure to give your guests good directions to your chosen spot.

Supplies for your party should include:

- Grill
- Charcoal
- Matches and lighter fluid
- Grilling utensils
- Folding chairs
- Tablecloth and blankets
- Cooler and thermos

The Menu and Activities

Plan a simple menu two days before the outing, and make a list of items to take. (See the following sample menu and list.) Pack the nonperishable items the night before, including the paper supplies (cups, plates, napkins, and paper towels). Remember to pack a small first aid kit, trash bags, wag bags, bottled water, and moist towelettes to clean your hands and the canines' paws.

For the main course for doggies and people, cook hot dogs and chili (prepare canine chili for doggies without spices, tomatoes, and onions). Suggestions for side dishes

Facing page: America's Top Dog Model 2008, Daphne Simone poses on her Astin Martin convertible. Nice wheels!

are nacho dip with chips for people, multigrain treats for doggies, and fall-themed treats from your local doggy bakery (e.g., footballs, pumpkins, turkeys, and leaves). To drink, provide beer and hot apple cider for people and bottled water for everyone. A delicious dessert that canines and people can enjoy is carob brownies. And don't forget the condiments for your human friends: ketchup, mustard, pickles, and relish.

Food should be ready to serve an hour before the game starts. This allows plenty of time for those attending the game to eat, help clean up, and extinguish fires. Those not attending the game can pull out a portable TV and dogsit. Enjoy the food and the frolic, and let the games begin!

Left: Romeo enjoys some sporty outdoor time at a "tail" gate party.
Facing page: Makaylah is dressed for an autumn outing.

Howl-O-Ween Party

The Howl-O-Ween Party can be a diva doggy's favorite soiree. What smart pooch doesn't like tricks and treats? Especially the treats. With the right preparation, most doggies embrace this ghoulish night in full regalia. Here's how to throw a wildly wicked Howl-O-Ween party, from slime green witch's brew to yummy snake pit stew!

The Setting

Send invitations to all of your favorite dog-owning partygoers four weeks before the festivities.

A week before the party, bring out the Halloween decorations that you have stored, and decorate the house. Shop for additional decorations if necessary.

The day before the party, set up the treat table with two tablecloths, one black and the other orange. Layer them so you can see both colors. Paint six orange metal buckets with black cats and bats. Fill buckets to overflowing with doggy treats. In front of the buckets, place prestuffed cellophane bags of doggy treats tied with black and orange ribbons. If the owner of your local pet boutique is savvy, he or she will have lots of Halloween treats in the bakery case to choose from. In each bucket of treats, place an orange and black Halloween mask made with a paper plates and glued to a paint stirrer.

Set up a buffet table for human guests as well. Cover the table with a spider web tablecloth that you have created or purchased.

Arrange jack-o'-lanterns around the entrance or along the walkway to light up the guests' path to your door.

The Menu and Activities

This spooky, scrumptious spread will scare up compliments fast! Advertise this menu on a blackboard (decorated with ghosts and goblins):

- Deviled ham bat sandwiches
- Snake pit stew (chili with sausage links cut in strips)
- Cornbread dogs
- Witch's brew (green punch)
- Great pumpkin cake

Doggies will flip for the bat sandwiches and snaky stew (minus spices, tomatoes, and onions).

You are invited to a Howl-O-Ween Party

If you can do the monster mash

Amble over to our Howl-O-Ween bash

Wear a mask and costume too

Dress up doggies just like you

Come at 6 o'clock and don't be late

The rest of the evening we'll leave to fate

Fright

Does your dog hate Halloween? It's not that uncommon, and many dog owners dread the arrival of masked strangers ringing their doorbells at all hours of the evening. Some dogs panic at the sight of their owners in baseball caps or dressy hats. If your diva dog considers the All Hallows Eve a true "fright night," you may have to spend some time acclimating him to the sight of you wearing a hat or a mask a few weeks before the party. Building up your dog's confidence is a good thing, and in no time he'll be enjoying the excitement and fun of a well-planned Howl-O-Ween party.

Keep water bowls filled to cool their tongues!

After the guests have devoured the feast, parade the doggies around the backyard. If you don't have a yard sizeable enough for a parade, take them to a park for the parade. Award a prize for the best doggy costume.

At the witching hour of your choosing, assemble all guests for a howling good time of trick or treat in the neighborhood.

Facing page: Maya and Pumpkin are ready to kick it up at a Howl-O-Ween bash!

Jingle Bell Dog Walk

The Jingle Bell Doggy Walk is a special opportunity to celebrate the Christmas holiday and support dog charities. Get into the holiday spirit by coordinating this event with your local humane society, an animal rescue league, or another fave dog charity.

The Setting

You may want to consider partnering with a local pet business owner who will likely have an extensive network of customers and supporters. As this is a grand event, you'll want to form a committee and solicit volunteers to help bring this jolly holiday cavalcade to life. There's a lot to consider, from applying for local permits, coordinating with law enforcement, and proper collection of donations to all the fun details of the walk, the music, and so forth.

The possibilities for a Jingle Bell Doggy Walk are endless, but the announcement on the following page serves as a sample of what could be possible with heaps of dedication and creativity:

National Pet Charities

American Humane Association, www.americanhumane.org
Angel on a Leash, www.angelonaleash.org
ASPCA, www.aspca.org
Best Friends Animal Society, www.bestfriends.org
Humane Society of the United States, www.hsus.org
Much Love Animal Rescue, www.muchlove.org
Noah's Wish, www.noahswish.org
The National Disaster Search Dog Foundation, www.searchdogfoundation.org
Take the Lead, www.takethelead.org
The Seeing Eye, www.seeingeye.org

Facing page: Jingle all the way . . . to a really festive holiday event!

Sample Event Invitation

'Tis the season for doggone fun!

Calling all canines and their people for a walk down Main Street
to benefit the [local chapter of the] Humane Society.

The street will be going to the dogs,
Saturday, December_____, _____, at 1 p.m.

- Registration for the Jingle Bell Doggy Walk will begin at 10 a.m. at the shelter.
- The registration fee is $_____ per doggy and $_____ for each additional dog and his people.
- During registration, you and your pooch will be entertained with games, live music, a flea market, food, and drink. Thanks to our many sponsors, there will be great dog- and people-watching and lots of doggy gifts.
- Participating doggies and their people will receive a Jingle Bell Doggy Walk T-shirt, doggy bag, and jingle bells for the walk.
- Pet photos with Santa Paws will be available for $_____.
- The walk will begin at _____Street and continue north on _____Street for a five-mile round-trip. There will be marked vehicles traveling the route for emergency transportation. Water for doggies and their people is available at stops along the way.

This is your opportunity to participate in a fun-filled day while supporting your local humane society. Please plan to come to this special holiday event.

Angel is decked out for the holidays.

Yappy New Year's Party

Bark in the New Year while sharing a festive, hearty supper with the ones you love. Fill your home with your closest canine friends and their people.

The Setting

On the invitation, print party details in red ink. Enclose the invitation in a white envelope and seal with red wax. You can find old-fashioned sealing wax at a specialty stationer, a gift store, or even a large bookstore. Be sure the invitation outlines the evening's festivities: guests arrive at 9 p.m. for cocktails and hors d'oeuvres, a lobster dinner served at 10 p.m., followed by a cheese course, a special homemade dessert at 11 p.m., and champagne at midnight to greet the New Year. Ask female guests and doggies to wear red. Gentlemen can wear red ties or bowties.

Decorate your front porch with red holiday lights. Red candles will set the right tone; freeze candles before burning for less drip and slower burn. On a special night such as New Year's Eve, the table setting will the main attraction. Make it glowingly perfect so that your guests feel special. A white linen tablecloth and red cloth napkins tied with gold ribbon set a festive tone. Line the center of the table from one end to the other with red votives and white pillars wrapped in gold ribbon.

Designate a room for your canine guests. If you have a few red blankets to pick up the red motif, that would be wonderful.

Menu

You will need a fabulous spread for this party. Here's a suggested menu for the various courses:

Drinks: Wine, champagne, and champagne cocktails for people; champagne (bottled water) for doggies

Hors d'oeuvres: Caviar for people; cheese twists for doggies

Salad: Caesar salad for people

Entrée: Broiled lobster tails and twice-baked potatoes for people; turkey meatballs for doggies

Cheese course: Three or four kinds of distinctive cheese—perhaps a soft

Facing page: New Year's Eve should be a formal event, served up with class and lots of bubbly.

mild cheese, a hard sharp cheese, and a blue cheese (such as gorgonzola or Stilton)—for everyone

Dessert: Miniature hot chocolate cakes for people; carob pupcakes for doggies

Countdown

Here is the countdown for party preparation:

Four weeks: send invitations, decorate house for the holidays.

Two weeks: select music, purchase candles, ribbons, and table décor.

One week: order cheese twists and carob pupcakes from the doggy bakery.

Two days: buy groceries for dinner.

One day: make (or purchase) hot chocolate cakes. Chill wine and champagne. Set table.

Four hours: make turkey meatballs.

Three hours: assemble dry ingredients for Caesar salad. Set up bar. Turn on outside red light.

Two hours: get yourself and doggy red-y.

Thirty minutes: put on music, light candles, reheat potatoes.

During champagne cocktails: set up cheese tray, broil lobster; toss salad with dressing.

During cheese course: prepare desserts.

After desserts: pour each guest a glass of champagne for the midnight toast. Fill doggy bowls with doggy champagne, then watch them yap in the New Year!

Y-A-P-P-Y N-E-W Y-E-A-R!!

Left: Spare no expense when dressing for the big night.
Facing page: Maya, Pumpkin, Romeo, and Makaylah are a dashing quartet, ready for the countdown!

Chapter 3

Doggy Spa and Pampering

A well-groomed pooch is welcome almost anywhere. A weekly visit to a doggy spa is a must for that perfect polished look. It will also provide your doggy with confidence and a feeling of well-being.

Right: Dress the part. Live the life.
Facing page: Fifey has no qualms about excessive pampering and primping.

At the Spa

Prior to scheduling a spa appointment, request an initial consultation to discuss your pet's needs and desires. Select a groomer who is experienced in all areas of the grooming process. A professional groomer will make an assessment of your pet's needs and then create a customized spa package.

A full-day spa package may include the following services: specialty treatments (bathing and conditioning), blow-dry, massage, brush, trim, style, pedicure, tooth brushing, ear cleaning, flea treatments, deodorizing, day care, and lunch.

Most spas offer an à la carte menu of remedies and treatments for those weekly maintenance needs. Health-conscious pet owners can choose products that are chemical-free, with only natural ingredients.

There are many doggy pampering products to choose from. Among the spectacular treatments that will pamper pets from head to tail are shampoos, leave-in moisturizers, vitamin-enriched conditioners, deodorants, tooth whiteners, breath mints, coat brighteners, ear creams, paw balm, nail polish, anti-aging treatments, stress-relief spray, and products containing essential oil and organic ingredients.

Today's spas allow your pet to visit while you are away on vacation. And many of the latest spas offer limo service to pick up and drop off your precious pooch. Those who do not wish to leave their pets behind while vacationing can take advantage of the many prestigious hotels that now offer fur-friendly spa services. You can visit the hotel spa for a relaxing and rejuvenating day for two.

Facing page: Poodles rule at Chateau Poochie. Jersey's ensconced in the Ruby Suite.

At the Beauty Parlor

Diva dogs who are particular about their looks can benefit from a makeover at a local beauty parlor.

Ultimate Makeover

Step one: A leisurely bath using natural shampoo and conditioner
Step two: Blow-dry, trim, and latest hairstyle
Step three: Pedicure complete with clipping, filing, and polish in a fab color
Step four: Teeth whitener and breath freshener
Step five: A bow or barrette that reflects the client's sense of style

Every young Yorkie's got to work it!

Choosing the right stylist and color can be exhausting.

The popular expression "beauty is only skin deep" could not be closer to the truth when talking about glamorous pooches. Yet, by feeling confident about her appearance, a blossoming goddess dog can develop her inner diva with the self assurance she needs to be almost anything. Be a top dog model. Be an accomplished athlete. Be a doggy celebrity. Be anything her heart desires!

Famous Doggies with Style

Asta, the dog star of the Thin Man films

America's Top Dog Model® winners, Linda, Mia, & Daphne Simone

Lassie

Toto

Wishbone

Facing page: Daisy is ready for her close-up.

Pumpkin enjoys some well-deserved down time in the Jade Suite at Chateau Poochie.

A Healthy Environment

The health of your well-pampered pooch should always be a consideration for devoted owners. Some spas offer advice on nutrition, diet, exercise, and anti-aging. Like the humans who own them, dogs are living longer. It is not uncommon for a dog to live beyond twelve years. Information on the latest health care products may be obtained from your vet or dog groomer.

Preventive health products for your pet are readily available, including dental care products, sunscreen, doggles (doggy sunglasses), vitamins, minerals, allergy medications, natural cuisine, weight loss plans, massage, doga (doggy yoga), and aromatherapy.

Preventive health care should be extended to home life as well. Diva dogs should be committed to maintaining a serene environment at home, filling corners with fresh fragrant flowers for aromatherapy, setting the tone with the glow of candlelight, and infusing the air with a signature scent.

Wise divas know that spending time in meditation and relaxation are keys to alleviating stress and promoting inner and outer beauty. That means let sleeping divas lie.

Being perceptive to your doggy's needs is a part of being a good dog parent. Choose products of good quality that will promote a long, healthy life for your pampered pooch. Following are tips for a healthy, pampered lifestyle.

Romeo is the picture of good health and exquisite taste.

Schedule a full physical exam for your dog at your veterinary clinic and find out which vitamins and minerals may be necessary for your doggy. Schedule annual dental visits to ensure healthy gums and teeth. Brush your dog's teeth at least three times a week.

Keep doggy's china bowl filled with bottled water. Visit the local dog bakery for fresh baked multigrain biscuits and natural treats. Avoid store-bought treats that may contain harmful chemicals and additives.

Apply sunscreen to doggy's nose and tummy prior to daytime outdoor activity. Make sure your dog wears protective doggles.

Investigate alternative therapies for your dog, such as acupuncture, herbal remedies, and homeopathic treatments. Take your doggy to doga for stress relief and total relaxation.

Schedule the royal treatment at a chic spa at least once a month. Consider sending doggy to the spa via pet limo to prep for special occasions. If you feel up to the task of bathing your dog at home, be sure to get all the best natural shampoos, conditioners, and sprays from your favorite pet boutique.

Arrange a getaway at a posh pet resort, complete with room service and complimentary doggy cham-

Who can resist the allure of the great outdoors?

pagne, massage, and dog walking/dog sitting service.

Stay connected! Remember to attach PetsCELL to your pooch's collar. In case of separation, your doggy can phone home!

These helpful tips will have every pampered pooch lapping up a life of luxury.

Chapter 4

The Rules of Petiquette

Training is a positive way to spend quality time with your precious pooch. It will create a lasting bond of mutual respect and ultimately benefit you, your family, and even your community. Bookstores and libraries are stocked with helpful manuals on dog training. Keep in mind that training should never be tedious or boring. It should be customized for style and doggone fun!

Petiquette is an important part of doggy training. The grand dames of etiquette, Emily Post and Amy Vanderbilt, remain the standard (and rightly so—preserved in those timeless volumes is a wealth of information worth heeding). For those diva dogs who have not attended finishing school, or had a debut, and haven't a Blue's Clue about how to walk or sit like a lady, here are some tips.

Petiquette starts at home. It is through house rules as well as play, fun, and games that diva dogs learn some of life's important lessons.

Facing page: At the Chesterfield Palm Beach, Jolly imagines himself the concierge who greets every proper canine guest.

Playdate Etiquette

A refined diva dog will be the first to welcome a new dog into the neighborhood. Invite the newcomer and her owner to your home for an afternoon visit and playdate. Be a good host or hostess by serving your canine guest (and her owner) first and offering them the most toothsome treats. Natural biscuits for your four-footed guest will impress both pooch and owner. Your neighbor may enjoy some homemade biscotti and a glass of ice wine.

During the playdate, be sure to have your diva dog share all of her treasures with her new playmate. At the end of the visit, if your pooch's new friend has been well behaved, offer her a bone for the road. A gift of a new ball or a bow to compliment your guest pooch's hairdo would be a classy touch. Let the newcomers know they are welcome back anytime. With any luck (and a little class!), they'll reciprocate and invite you to their doggy pad for the next visit.

Never drink too much on the first date.

Facing page: No matter how gorgeous she is, don't let Daphne Simone take the Jag to her playdate.

Good Conversation

Another important part of petiquette is being a good conversationalist. One doesn't mouth a new friend's muzzle mid-sentence! A good conversationalist is articulate, discreet, and considerate. A properly trained diva dog doesn't bark with her mouth full of liver. She makes friends feel comfortable by not discussing such topics as politics and religion and saving insecurities and complaints for therapy. This of course goes for owners as well! Here is a crash course in how to bark without being a boor:

- Do listen attentively with ears perked up.
- Do not bark loudly; use your indoor voice.
- Do take pleasure in enjoying your meal without slurping.
- Do insist upon the best treats from the dog bakery.
- Do not interrupt unless it's an emergency that can only be resolved outside.
- Do be pawsitive, dahling!

Resist the temptation to make the conversation all about you.

Facing page: Try though he did, Romeo couldn't make sparkling conversation with his new playmate.

Wedding Etiquette

It's important to know the protocol for all occasions, the most important of these, of course, being the wedding. This is a very big day in a diva dog's life. Because of puppy love and doggy infatuation, dog weddings have become commonplace in the dog world. We would like to think that puppy love conquers all, but in reality it sometimes requires expert advice in the form of a wedding planner, a caterer, and a dog-fearing minister to handle the ceremony itself. This is a real opportunity for diva dogs to exchange bow-wow vows that are meant to last a lifetime.

The entire event requires a lot of time and preparation. A wedding is never an occasion to be frugal or pawsimonious! Your diva only gets married once, so give her the big day she's always dreamt about.

When it comes to the bride and groom, there are a lot of resources available, but guests are often left in the dark! For instance, wedding fashions are forever changing.

Some things do remain the same, however. Here is what we know for sure about attending a wedding:

- Never wear white! Even if the bride wears black!
- Don't forget the wrap in sacred places. Save bare shoulders for the reception.
- Hats are for daytime. Wear a hat only to a day wedding.
- Wear fashions made of fabric appropriate for the season.
- Be prepared to celebrate—wear something fit to romp and roll!

Wobbles and Wiggles rehearse their nuptials in chic attire.

Must-Know Rules

There are so many things to learn in a diva dog's life. It's all about good breeding. These twenty-five must-know rules of petiquette will ensure that your adorable darling is trained for every situation:

Everyday Living!

Rule number 1: Obey the rules of the house—doghouse, that is!

Rule number 2: Respect your parents. Learn not to bark back.

Rule number 3: Learn at a young age where not to do your business.

Rule number 4: Graciously accept praise for good behavior—accept gourmet treats, too!

Rule number 5: Never give canine friends the run of the house. Not even if your owner has pet insurance.

Rule number 6: Get to know the new dog in the neighborhood. Schedule a playdate.

Rule number 7: Females should learn to walk and sit like a lady.

Rule number 8: Follow a scent only if it's a good-smelling one!

Rule number 9: Don't howl just because your neighbor is howling.

Rule number 10: If you are born into fame, learn how to avoid the puparazzi.

For Appearance's Sake

Rule number 11: Maintain a perfect pet-i-cure. Insist that your owner keep your nails neatly trimmed and polished.

Rule number 12: Attend a weekly doggy massage, followed by a shampoo and style.

Rule number 13: Practice good grooming. Instruct your owner to brush your hair 100 strokes daily!

Rule number 14: Have good scents-ability. Use Sexy Beast haute perfume for dogs.

Rule number 15: Be sure your human is subscribing to one or all of the following: *Dog Fancy*, *Modern Dog*, *Animal Fair*, and other chic publications for the latest styles.

Rule number 16: Wear your Cartier dog tag and Mikimoto pearls only on special occasions.

Rule number 17: Find a good dog tailor. Clothing should fit properly to flatter your figure and for your own safety.

Rule number 18: Watch *Celebrity Pet Dish*, *The Oprah Winfrey Show*, and *Animal Planet* to keep on top.

Bullet is on target to be the life of the party.

Rule number 19: Walk at least three times a day for exercise and weight maintenance.

Rule number 20: Drink eight china bowls of bottled water daily, but beware of accidents!

Rule number 21: Present yourself like the pampered pooch that you are!

Social Life

Rule number 22: Attend only the most fabulous doggy parties, the ones that quickly become the talk of town and country.

Rule number 23: Listen to music about yourself: "Puppy Love" and *Songs to Make Dogs Happy*.

Rule number 24: Share your owner by letting him or her get involved in the community.

Rule number 25: Be sure your owner is on top of all your social engagements with America's Top Dog Model calendar.

As wise as any diva dog, Daisy never leaves home without it!

Resources

Accessories

California

Diva Dog
4850 La Cruz Place
San Diego, CA 91941
Tel: 866-825-6666

Doggles, LLC
6160 Enterprise Dr., Unit G
Diamond Springs, CA 95619
Tel: 530-344-1645
www.doggles.com

Hedy Manon
537 Newport Center Dr., Suite 305
Newport Beach, CA 92660
Tel: 800-755-1546
www.hedymanon.com

Florida

Sherry Frankel's Melangerie
256 Worth Ave.
Palm Beach, FL 33480
Tel: 561-655-1996

New York

Le Chien
Trump Plaza
1044 Third Ave.
New York, NY 10012
Tel: 800-LeChien
www.lechiennyc.com

Texas

Poochey Shoos
5930 Royal Lane, Suite E
PMB 228
Dallas, TX 75230
Tel: 972-386-0973
www.poocheyshoos.com

Worldwide

Burberry
Tel: 866-589-0499
www.burberry.com

Coach
Tel: 888-262-6224
www.coach.com

Gucci
Tel: 212-826-2600
www.gucci.com

Hermes
Tel: 800-441-1546
www.hermes.com

Juicy Couture
Tel: 888-908-1160
http://info.juicycouture.com

Louis Vuitton
Tel: 877-890-7171
www.louisvuitton.com

Bone Appétit

California

Cool Pets Raw Gourmet
2033 S. Hathaway St.
Santa Ana, CA 92705
Tel: 714-545-0700
www.coolpetsrawgourmet.com

Five Paw Bakery
315 Main St.
Los Altos, CA 94022
Tel: 650-941-5729
www.fivepaw.com

Kool Dog Kafe
1666 S. Pacific HWY
Redondo Beach, CA 90277
Tel: 310-944-3232
www.kooldogkafe.com

Scraps Dog Bakery
12034 Nevada City Hwy.
Grass Valley, CA 94510
Tel: 530-274-4493
www.scrapsdogbakery.net

Florida

Blu Dog Bakery
5084 Biscayne Blvd.
Miami, FL 33137
Tel: 305-754-0316

Star Barks/The Dog Treat Bakery
711 W. Indiantown Rd. #B8
Jupiter, FL 33458
Tel: 866-305-BARK
www.starbarksonline.com

Three Dog Bakery
5250 Town Center Circle
Boca Raton, FL 33486
Tel: 561-347-8771
www.threedog.com

Missouri

Three Dog Bakeries
World Dog Quarters
1843 N. Topping Ave.
Kansas City, MO 64120
Tel: 800-4-TREATS
www.threedog.com
Nationwide locations

Treats Unleashed
36 Clarkson Wilson Center
Chesterfield, MO 63017
Tel: 636-536-5900
www. treats-unleashed.com

Nevada

Duke's Natural Food & Bakery
4130 S. Sandhill Rd.
Las Vegas, NV 89121
Tel: 702-458-7931

Flea Bags Bakery & Bowtique
2225 Village Walk Dr. Suite 173
Henderson, NV 89052
Tel: 702-914-8805

New York

Bone Appétit Bakery
340 Jericho Turnpike
Syosset, NY 11791
Tel: 877-619-7387
www.tastypettreats.com

Buttercup's Paw-Tisserie
63 Fifth Ave.
Brooklyn, NY 11217
Tel: 718-399-2228
www.buttercupspaw.com

Oklahoma

Dog Dish
6502 E. 51st St.
Tulsa, OK 74145
Tel: 918-624-2600
www.thedogdish.com

South Carolina

Pupcakes Boutique & Bakery
3211 Devine St.
Columbia, SC 29205
Tel: 803-471-0236

Tailwaggers
1 N. Forest Beach Dr.
Hilton Head Island, SC 29928
Tel: 843-836-5276
www.tail-waggers.com

Texas

Groovy Dog Bakery
4477 S. Lamar, Suite 580
Austin, TX 78703
Tel: 866-GroovyDog
www.groovydogbakery.com

Virginia

Olde Towne Bakery
11105 Leavells Rd., Suite 5
Fredricksburg, VA 22407
Tel: 540-710-0012

Washington

Railey's Leash & Treat
513 N. 36th St.
Seattle, WA 98103
Tel: 206-632-5200
www.raileys.com

Wisconsin

Katzenbarkers
112 Clark St.
Wausau, WI 54401
Tel: 715-845-9191

Canine Couture

Alabama

Fetch Boutique
601 Greensboro Ave.
Tuscaloosa, AL 35401
Tel: 205-247-5476
www.qpluxury.com

Alaska

Bubba's Dog Walking
8307 Duben Ave.
Anchorage, AK 99504
Tel: 907-351-2004

Arizona

My Puppy's Closet
19402 N. 31st St. Way
Phoenix, AZ 85050
Tel: 602-430-4591

Paws and Claws Boutique
3061 N. Campbell Ave.
Tucson, AZ 85719
Tel: 520-795-7297
www.pawsandclawsonline.com

California

Doggie Styles
9467 Charleville Blvd.
Beverly Hills, CA 90212
310-278-0031
www.doggiestylesonline.com

Barkus Pet Boutique
5225 Canyon Crest Dr., #17C
Riverside, CA 92507
Tel: 951-788-5845
www.barkuspet.com

Fifi & Romeo Boutique
7282 Beverly Blvd.
Los Angeles, CA 90036
Tel: 323-857-7214

Hollywood Hounds
8218 W. Sunset Blvd.
Los Angeles, CA 90046
Tel: 323-650-5551
www.hollywoodhounds.com

Paw Boutique
523 S. Raymond
Pasadena, CA 91105
Tel: 626-394-0946

Ruff Ruff and Meow
17945 Sky Park Circle, Suite E
Irvine, CA 92614
Tel: 866-742-RUFF
www.ruffruffandmeow.com

Colorado

CB Paws
420 Hyman Ave. Mall
Aspen, CO 81611
Tel: 970-925-5848
www.cbpaws.com

CB Paws
278 Fillmore St.
Denver, CO 80206
Tel: 877-616-PAWS
www.cbpaws.com

Connecticut

Perfectly Spoiled Pet
125 Broad St.
Milford, CT 06460
Tel: 203-701-0753

Florida

Bibi's Boutique
250 Worth Ave.
Palm Beach, FL 33480
Tel: 561-823-1973
www.bibisplayhouse.com

Downtown Dogs
1631 Snow Ave.
Tampa, FL 33606
Tel: 813-250-DOGS
www.shopdowntowndogs.com

Gigi & Luca Pet Boutique
1825 NE 24th St.
Lighthouse Point, FL 33064
Tel: 954-784-8755
www.gigiandluca.com

Herringbone & Hound
888 East Las Olas Blvd.
Ft. Lauderdale, FL 33301
Tel: 954-768-0420

Waggs To Riches
505 East Atlantic Ave.
Delray Beach, FL 33483
Tel: 561-272-8100
www.waggstoriches.com

Lap of Luxury
16850 Jog Road, Suite 107
Delray Beach, FL 33446
Tel: 561-637-3856

Sniffany & Company
3240 SW 34th St., Suite 706
Ocala, FL 34474
Tel: 352-857-9318

Chateau Poochie
4301 N. Federal Hwy.
Lighthouse Point, FL 33064
Tel: 954-561-8111
www.chateaupoochie.com

Teacups Puppies & Boutique
3180 Sterling Rd.
Hollywood, FL 33021
Tel: 954-985-8848
www.teacupspuppies.com

Hawaii

Paw-parazzi
744 Front St., #4
Maui, HI 96761
Tel: 808-662-0624

Idaho

Charley the Pet Boutique
160 North 8th St.
Boise, ID 83703
Tel: 208-331-6605

Illinois

Tails in the City
One East Delaware Place
Chicago, IL 60611
Tel: 312-649-0347
www.tailsinthecity.com

Michigan

Chic Pet Boutique
1400 Lakeside Circle
Sterling Heights, MI 48315
Tel: 586-566-4933
www.chicpetboutique.net

Minnesota

LuLu & Luigi
3844 Grand Way
St. Louis Park, MN 55416
Tel: 952-929-5858

LuLu & Luigi
813 East Lake Street
Wayzata, MN 55391
Tel: 952-929-5858 (LuLu)
www.luluandluigi.com

Nebraska

Luxe Pet Boutique
16950 Wright Plaza, Suite 151
Omaha, NE 68130
Tel: 402-502-0282
www.luxepetboutique.com

Nevada

Haute Diggity Dog
1591 Buffalo, Suite 110
Las Vegas, NV 89128
Tel: 702-257-0213
www.hautediggitydog.com

Lush Puppy
3930 Las Vegas Blvd., Suite 128
South Las Vegas, NV 89119
Tel: 702-740-2254
www.lushpuppyonline.com

New York

Canine Styles
830 Lexington Ave.
New York, NY 10021
Tel: 212-838-2064
www.caninestyles.com

Canine Styles Downtown
43 Greenwich Ave.
New York, NY 10014
Tel: 212-352-8591

Canine Styles Uptown
1195 Lexington Ave.
New York, NY 10038
Tel: 212-472-9440

Hampton Hound
2485 Montauk Hwy
Bridgehampton, NY 11932
Tel: 631-537-7650
www.hamptonshound.com

Le Chien Dog Boutique
Trump Plaza
1044 Third Ave.
New York, NY 10012
Tel: 800-LeChien
www.lechiennyc.com

Trixie & Peanut
23 E. 20th St.
New York, NY 10003
Tel: 888-838-6780

Ohio

Doggie Foo Foo
12675 Millview Lane

Chardon, OH 44024
Tel: 440-537-3697
www.doggiefoofoo.com

Texas

Fifi and Fidos Pet Boutique
555 E. Basses Rd., Suite 111
San Antonio, TX 78209
Tel: 210-822-2525

Glamour Dog
2693 Preston Rd., Suite 1010
Frisco, TX 75034
Tel: 972-335-1030
www.glamourdog.com

Virginia

Cha-Cha Couture
860 Woodstock Rd.
Virginia Beach, VA 23454
Tel: 757-961-0514
www.cha-chacouture.com

Virgin Islands

How 'Bout Your Pet
22 Dronningens Gade
St. Thomas, VI 00802
Tel: 340-777-1130
www.howboutyourpet.com

Washington

Urban Dogs Bellevue
2036 Bellevue Square
Bellvue, WA 98004
Tel: 425-456-0009
www.urban-dogs.com

Urban Dogs Tacoma
1717 Dock St.
Tacoma, WA 98402
Tel: 253-573-1717

Nationwide

Juicy Couture
http://info.juicycouture.com

Target Stores
www.target.com

Canada

Bark & Fitz
5674 Monkland Ave.
Montreal, QC H3Z 1H1
Tel: 514-483-3555

Poochey Couture
TMR Shopping Centre
2344 Lucerne
Montreal, QC H3R 2J8
Tel: 866-440-K999

England

Harrods
87-135 Brampton Rd.
Knights Bridge
London SW1X7XL
Tel: 020-7730-1234
www.harrods.com

France

Galeries Lafayette
40, Bd. Haussman
75009 Paris, France
Tel: 01-42-82-34-56
www.galerieslafayette.com

Germany

Cane e Gatto
Englishal Kinger Strasse 245
D-81927 Munich, Germany
Tel: 49-89-99-34-19-19
www.caneegatto.de

Japan

Bul Bu-Bu
The Tokyo Meguro-ku
Greenery Stand 1-13-11
Lilac House 2F
Tokyo, Japan
Tel: 03-3463-0151
www.bulbubu.com

Dogbase Az Heart
Honmoku 231-0821
Main Maki Field
Yokohama City, Japan
Tel: 045-623-4911
www.azheart.jp

Tanti Baci
Osaka City North
Ku Hall Island, 2 Chome
1-27 Cherry Bridge, Bldg. 2F
Chiyoda, Japan
Tel: 043-543-0003
www.tantibaci.jp

Tiara Pets
Tiara Co., Ltd.
5-13-17 Kiminomori-minami, Ohamishirasato,
Sanbu, Chiba, Japan 299-3241
Tel: 047-553-3552
www.tiarapets.com

Netherlands

Pet Design
Vughterstraat 56 5211
GK Den Bosch
The Netherlands
Tel: 31-736132364
www.petdesign.nl

Worldwide

Burberrys
Tel: 866-589-0499
www.burberry.com

Gucci
Tel: 212-826-2600
www.gucci.com

Ralph Lauren
Tel: 888-475-7674
www.ralphlauren.com

Dog Publications

Animal Fair
www.animalfair.com

Bark
www.thebark.com

Dog Fancy
www.dogchannel.com/
dfdc_portal.aspx

Dog World
www.dogchannel.com/dog-magazine/
dogworld

Modern Dog
www.moderndogmagazine.com

Pet Style News
www.petstylenews.com

Fine Pet Jewelry

Andrea Levine Jewelry
Independence Mall
1601 Concord Pike
Suites #38 A & B
Wilmington, DE 19803
Tel: 866-912-7333

Dorothy Bauer Designs
702 Harrison St., Unit A
Berkeley, CA 94710
Tel: 800-531-3087
www.dorothybauer.com

Doggie Dreamhouse Builder

La Petite Maison
Tel: 877-404-1184
www.lapetitemaison

Elegant Pet Stationery

The Pet Set
97 Grand Blvd.
Emerson, NJ 07630
Tel: 201-225-1307
www.the-petset.com

National Animal Protection

Humane Society of the United States
2100 L St. NW
Washington, DC 20037
Tel: 202-452-1100
www.hsus.org

Pet Insurance

Veterinary Pet Insurance (VPI)
Tel: 800-989-6552
www.petinsurance.com/hsus

PetsCell

PetsMobility Networks, Inc.
10575 114th St. Suite 2
Tel: 480-344-7724
Tel: 888-884-PETS
www.petsmobility.com

Premier Pet Friendly Hotels

Beverly Hills Plaza Hotel
10300 Wilshire Boulevard
Los Angeles, California 90024
Tel: 310-275-5575
www.beverlyhillsplazahotel.com

Grove Isle Hotel & Spa
Four Grove Isle Drive
Coconut Grove (Miami), FL 33133
Tel: 800-844-7683
www.groveisle.com

Kimpton Hotels Nationally
Tel: 800-KIMPTON
www.kimptonhotels.com

Loews Hotels Nationally
Tel: 800-23-LOEWS
www.loewshotels.com

Nine Zero Hotel
90 Tremont St.
Boston, MA 02108
Tel: 866-906-9090
www.ninezero.com

The Peninsula Beverly Hills
9882 S. Santa Monica Blvd.
Beverly Hills, CA 90212
Tel: 800-462-7899
www.beverlyhills.peninsula.com

The Point
P.O. Box 1327
Saranac Lake, NY 12983
Tel: 800-255-3530
www.thepointresort.com

Rittenhouse Hotel
210 West Rittenhouse Square
Philadelphia, PA 19103
Tel: 800-635-1042
www.rittenhousehotel.com

San Ysidro Rancho
900 San Ysidro Lane
Santa Barbara, CA 93108
Tel; 800-368-6788
www.sanysidroranch.com

St. Regis Aspen
315 East Dean St.
Aspen, CO 81611
Tel: 888-454-9005
www.stregisaspen.com

Viceroy Palm Springs
415 S. Belardo Rd.

Palm Springs, CA 92262
Tel: 800-670-6814
www.viceroypalmsprings.com

W Hotels Worldwide
Tel: 877-946-8357
www.starwoodhotels.com/
whotels

Wyndham Peaks Resort & Golden Door Spa
136 Country Club Blvd.
Telluride, CO 81435
Tel: 800-789-2220
www.thepeaksresort.com

Scents of Style*

Apple & Mint Dog Lotion
Mango Mutt
www.mangomutt.co.uk

Aromatic Eau de Toilette
Pet Esthé
www.petesthe.com

Bone Soap-on-a-Rope
Cain & Able
www.cainandablecollection.com

Designer Dog Colognes
Doggie Vogue
www.doggievogue.com

Juicy Crittoure
Juicy Couture
http://info.juicycouture.com

Kiehl's for Your Dog
Kiehl's
www.kiehls.com

Lavender of Lulu Spritz
Lulu Jane
Available through various online retailers

Martine's Perfume
Le Chien
www.lechiennyc.com

Oh My Dog! Parfum
Dog Generation
www.doggeneration.com

Organic Botanical L
ani Spritz
Muttropolis
www.muttropolis.com

Spa Dog Botanicals
www.spadogbotanicals.com

* Products may vary

Spectacular Spas

California

A-1 LaunDro-Mutt
1921 De La Vina, Suite A
Santa Barbara, CA 93101
Tel: 805-687-2083

Bath & Biscuits
5635 Freeport Blvd., #7

Sacramento, CA 95822
Tel: 916-428-9274
www.bathandbiscuits.com

Bathe R Doggie
101 W. California Blvd.
Pasadena, CA 91105
Tel: 626-795-7777

Dog Beach Dog Wash
4933 Voltaire St. #C
San Diego, CA 92107
Tel: 619-523-1792
www.dogwash.com

Doggie in the Window
4106 E. Anaheim St.
Long Beach, CA 90804
Tel: 562-494-7085
www.doggieinthewindow.net

Dunk-N-Dogs
2178 Bush St.
San Francisco, CA 94115
Tel: 415-931-1108

Estrella Spa
Viceroy Palm Springs
415 S. Belardo Rd.
Palm Springs, CA 92262
Tel: 760-320-4117
Tel: 800-670-6184
www.viceroypalmsprings.com

Four Wet Feet
4599 18th St.
San Francisco, CA 94114
Tel: 415-701-PAWS

I Dig My Dog
2160 E. Foothill Blvd.

Pasadena, CA 91107
Tel: 626-844-7877
Tel: 800-844-7877
www.idigmydog.com

Nature's Grooming & Boutique
3110 Main St., Suite 104
Santa Monica, CA 90405
Tel: 310-392-8758
www.naturesgrooming.com

Tailwashers Pet Grooming
1929 N. Bronson Ave.
Hollywood, CA 90068
Tel: 323-464-9600
www.twaggers.com

Colorado

CB Paws
278 Fillmore St.
Denver, CO 80206
Tel: 303-322-PAWS
www.cbpaws.com

Florida

Chateau Poochie
4301 N. Federal Hwy.
Lighthouse Point, FL 33064
Tel: 954-561-3336
www.chateaupoochie.com

Groomingdales
10800 N. Military Trail, Suite 112
Palm Beach Gardens, FL 33410
Tel: 561-848-7400
www.groomingdales.com

Lap of Luxury
168 S. Jog Rd., Suite 107

Delray Beach, FL 33446
Tel: 561-637-3856

Pet Haven
1833 N.E. 24th St.
Lighthouse Point, FL 33064
Tel: 954-941-6315

Georgia

The Pet Set
2480 Briarcliff Rd.
Atlanta, GA 30329
Tel: 404-633-8755
www.thepetset.com

Illinois

Soggy Paws
1148 W. Leland Ave.
Chicago, IL 60640
Tel: 773-334-7663
www.soggypaws.com

Minnesota

LuLu & Luigi
Grooming Pawlour
812 E. Lake St.
Wayzata, MN 55391
Tel: 952-929-5858
www.luluandluigi.com

New York

Canine Ranch Spa
452A Columbus Ave.
New York, NY 10024
Tel: 212-595-PETS
Tel: 877-K-9-RANCH
www.canineranchnyc.com

Canine Ranch Spa
38 Park Place
East Hampton, NY 11937
Tel: 631-329-DOGS
www.canineranchnyc.com

Le Chien
Trump Plaza
1044 Third Ave.
New York, NY 10012
Tel: 800-LeChien
www.lechiennyc.com

New York Dog Spa & Hotel
32 W. 25th St.
New York, NY 10010
Tel: 212-243-1199
www.dogspa.com

Nevada

Barker Shop
6392 Aclare Ave.
Las Vegas, NV 89118
Tel: 702-362-3006

Desert Breeze Pet Grooming
3655 S. Durange Dr., Suite 16
Las Vegas, NV 89147
Tel: 702-256-6986

Pet Central Grooming
4250 E. Bonanza Rd.
Las Vegas, NV 89110
Tel: 702-437-9022
www.petcentralusa.com

Petiquette Pet Grooming
2654 W. Horizon Pkwy
Henderson, NV 89052
Tel: 702-258-7387

Pink Poodle Parlor Too
8866 S. Eastern Ave.
Las Vegas, NV 89123
Tel: 702-933-5729

Texas

Clip 'n Dip Grooming
10224 Midway Rd.
Dallas, TX 75229
Tel: 214-350-2547

Dunkin Doggie
718 N. Buckner Blvd.
Dallas, TX 75218
Tel: 214-321-5200

England

Pugs & Kisses
183 New Kings Rd., Fulham
London, England SW6 4SW
Tel: 0200-7731-0098
www.pugsandkisses.com

Japan

Dog Club 1st
B2 Lumine Est,
3-38-1 Shinjuku,
Shinjuku-ku, Tokyo
Japan
Tel: 03-5363-1162
www.dog1st.com

Training Dogs

National K-9 Dog Trainers Association
www.nk9dta.com

Association of Pet Dog Trainers (APDT)
www.apdt.com

Top Dog Contest

America's Top Dog Model
www.americastopdogmodel.com

Top Doggy Organizations

American Boarding Kennels Association
www.abka.com
American Canine Association
www.acacanines.com

American Kennel Club (AKC)
www.akc.org

American Pet Association
www.apapets.org

American Society for the Prevention of Cruelty to Animals
www.aspca.org

Guiding Eyes for the Blind
www.guiding-eyes.org

National Association of Professional Pet Sitters
www.petsitters.org

National Dog Groomers Association (NDGA)
www.nationaldoggroomers.com

Paws with a Cause
www.pawswithacause.org

Index